Advan

Pause: The Journal

"If you're like me, journaling can be therapeutic and healing. Pause: The Journal is no exception to that as a self-healing, wonderful way to think differently about today and what you choose to create. What better way to start my day than with *Pause: The Journal*."

- Barnet Bain,
director of *Milton's Secret*;
producer of *What Dreams May Come*;
author of *The Book of Doing and Being*

"Awakening your intuition is one of the most important ways to move into your place of inner peace and power. *Pause: The Journal* helps you do just that - by writing and following the daily prompts, you open space to reconnect with your inner knowing and put its wisdom into practice in your life. What better way to start living the life of your dreams!"

- Kim Chestney,
author of *Radical Intuition: A Revolutionary Guide to Using Your Inner Power*
and founder of *IntuitionLab*

"There is so much power in taking a pause. When we practice this consistently, our lives begin to feel more in alignment, more intentional, more fulfilling, and more juicy. *Pause: The Journal* guides us to start envisioning what our own miraculous day looks and feels like, and inspires us to take the courageous steps to get there. I highly recommend this journal as a dynamic daily regimen to help you create a life that lights you up!"

\- Kate Eckman,
award-winning author of *The Full Spirit Workout*

"What better way to pause, reflect, and align than to have a daily reflection practice. *Pause: The Journal* delivers on that. The powerful self-inquiry helps you to not only discover and reach your dreams, but to show up for what's required to help you get there.

\- Sage Lavine,
CEO of Women Rocking Business
and bestselling author of *Women Rocking Business*

"Bring on the pen! Rachael's beautiful journal provided prompts that helped me visualize what I want more of in my life. It's not always easy to know when life feels chaotic and overwhelming, but working through this journal, I feel calm, focused... and I even enjoyed the process! I'm so grateful for these tools—the world certainly needs more *pause*."

- Darcy Luoma, CEO and Master Certified Coach; author of *Thoughtfully Fit: Your Training Plan for Life & Success*

"Many think they can optimally navigate life without writing things down. *Pause: The Journal*, asks that we think again. By taking the time to write (even if it's for 2 minutes), we can change the wiring in our brain to bring more compassion, patience and positivity to our life. This journal is the optimal guide to show you how."

- Val Ries, Executive Coach and author of *Chief Inspiration Officer*

" Bravo! Rachael has done a masterful job at not just inspiring you to write, but also explaining exactly how to write so you get the most out of it. Many of my coaching clients have successfully used journaling to organize their thoughts so they can share them to feel more connected. The prompts in Chapter 3 are a perfect guide to help you uncover and express how you are really feeling."

- Rnold Smith, President & Chief Visionary at *Connection App*

Pause
The Journal

How to Use Intentional Writing

To Create Your Dreams

Rachael O'Meara

Grow Rich Publishing

Pause the Journal
How to Intentionally Write to Create Your Dreams
Rachael O'Meara

Pause for Ten Percent: Ten percent of all author royalties are
donated to "Pause-some" nonprofits annually.

Dedication

For the doers, the dreamers, the thinkers, and the writers who give themselves permission to pause.

This journal is an opportunity to pause so you can create the space to find your truth through the power of intentional writing.

I invite you, dear dreamer, to think big, and sink into the creative space to let your thoughts flow from mind to paper. What comes out may surprise you. It is in service to your becoming.

This is your blank slate to be, in service to your doing. These are your prompts to process, intend, be, and dream.

In this space is the power of pause to intentionally write in service to what you dream to create.

Contents

Without leaps of imagination or dreaming, we lose the excitement of possibilities.
Dreaming, after all, is a form of planning.

– GLORIA STEINEM

Foreword

Congratulations on beginning your pause journey! *Pause: The Journal* will help you form a new habit of taking daily breaks to read, write, and reflect.

During our information age we all suffer from some form of stress or feeling overwhelmed with social media updates, texts and news alerts on our smartphones, or simply juggling work, family and personal life. On top of that, it's easy to become addicted to our to-do lists and the busyness of life.

To combat such feelings, I begin every weekday writing in my journal, followed by a brief meditation. The self-critical, workaholic voice in my head almost always chimes in, telling me to instead get to work, yet I know how important it is to maintain those habits.

The act of writing by hand slows my mind down. I reflect on what I'm grateful for as well as my larger goals, objectives, and dreams. And meditation gets me into a calmer mindset, enabling me to achieve a deeper state of concentration. Done in tandem, I feel happier, more present, and ultimately, I can get more done with a clearer head. In addition, journaling and meditation have helped me become a better listener and friend to those around me.

But this wasn't always the case. During the Great Recession of 2009, I was laid off and found myself with the freedom to take a pause to do something that I'd scribbled on my bucket list: write a book. This sudden change forced me to stop and reflect and birthed my new life as a writer and consultant.

Then it all happened again! Six months after I started in a new job, the advertising agency I worked at lost a few clients and laid me off. So, I decided to write my second book and incorporate my own marketing consulting company.

My two "forced pauses" made me take a break and helped me discover the power of journaling. But now I choose to pause and write in my journal every weekday.

In 2017, Rachael O'Meara invited me to share my experience in her book, *Pause: Harnessing the Life-Changing Power of Giving Yourself a Break*. I had previously met Rachael at Fordham Business School after which she had lived through her own Pause, as described in her book. While working at Google, she took a leave of absence after experiencing burnout and returned three months later to Google with a fresh mindset. She continues collecting Pause stories and speaking with experts in her *Pausecast*, a podcast series featuring topics on the cutting edge of emotional intelligence, mindfulness, neuroscience, and human potential. Today, since leaving Google, she works with executives as a transformational leadership coach helping them to rise to their next level in their professional or personal lives.

When we allow ourselves the opportunity to create a space of calm for ourselves – in this case, to journal – we can intentionally shift our behavior, get closer to our dreams and ultimately live the life we want to live. This is the gift of *Pause: The Journal*. Rachael teaches you the skills to ensure that your one precious life is filled with what you want in it. In journaling, you're sending a message to the universe that you prioritize your own dreams and goals. You're investing in yourself. Let's begin!

Joe Kutchera
Founder of Latino Link Advisors
author of Latino Link and E-X-I-T-O

Introduction

I am thrilled you found *Pause: The Journal* (or maybe it found you!). Consider this sacred space between what's present for you TODAY, and who you want to become.

It's been my intention from the get-go, ever since the book *Pause: Harnessing the Life-Changing Power of Giving Yourself a Break* was published, to provide an accompanying journal to write down your thoughts in the here and now, so that you can process them and use them as momentum to move forward in the direction of who you could become. In other words, a place to track what's going on with you and a space to think beyond what's happening in your life.

I can't think of a better tool to do this than intentional writing. And that's what journaling really is; it's conscious writing! It is also merging your unconscious thoughts and feelings with what is conscious to you as words go from your mind to the paper.

Whether you've read the book *Pause*, listened to *The Pausecast* podcast, or been a coaching client, you likely know that journaling is one of the most effective daily pauses you can do. Now, it's time to put the rubber to the road, or the pen to the paper, in this case, and intentionally write.

Chapter 1

Why Journaling Matters

I write to discover what I know. — Flannery O'Connor

If you are already a journal fan, chances are you don't need additional info on why journaling matters. For you journaling geeks like me, here's a bit more information and the top benefits on why it's so important to have journaling as one of your channels to think, feel, and process.

Here are the incredible benefits of journaling and why it's such a power tool:

• **Your well-being and mood can improve.** Research tells us that journaling for as little as two minutes on two consecutive days about an emotionally significant event improves mood and well-being (1).

- **Design Your Future.** Writing about your experiences or envisioning how you want to feel or what you desire to create is a terrific way to be intentional with yourself and set yourself up for success.

- **Become more present.** By noting what you experience or want to experience in your day, you are staying present. Not only can you describe what you did or want to do today, you can share what happened. Were you excited, nervous, or hungry? How did it make you feel? Maybe you want to free-form draw and see what appears. Blank pages (or "blank slates" as I like to call them here) are excellent for this practice.

- **Activate new neural circuitry.** The physical act of writing has a neurological effect on the brain. As Henriette Anne Klauser explains in *Write it Down, Make it Happen*, writing stimulates a bunch of cells in the brain called the "reticular activating system" or RAS, which in turn signals the cerebral cortex in the brain to wake up and pay attention (2). The same thing happens as you set your vision and orient towards what you want to achieve. Think of it like training your brain to spot evidence that you are on the right path, which helps you stay motivated and moving forward.

- **Access Your Innate Gifts.** Judith Blackstone, author of *Belonging Here: A Guide for the Spiritually Sensitive Person*, created a step-by-step guide to help readers be more here and now with what she calls the "Realization Process" (3). This process leverages an individual's innate physical and spiritual gifts. Blackstone makes the point that each of us can use our spiritual gifts as entryways into both the depths of human connection and our innermost selves. When you tap into this, your physical presence and engagement with others deepens.

- **Develop more self-compassion.** I'm reminded of Ram Dass, author of the 1971 classic *Be Here Now*. Journaling is a means to cultivate self-compassion by being with yourself at any given moment. Instead of holding the laundry list of to-dos for the day ahead, or worrying about what may not go right, instead, just write about it. Dass writes:

"Just be here now. Reflect on the thought that if you are truly Here and Now a) it is enough, and b) you will have optimum power and understanding to do the best thing at the given moment. Thus, when *then* (the future) becomes *Now* — if you have learned this discipline — you will then be in an ideal position to do the best thing. So, you need not spend your time worrying about *then*" (4).

- **Make more of your subconscious *conscious*.** Your unconscious mind is a million times more powerful than your conscious mind (5). Your conscious mind's prefrontal cortex alone processes forty nerve impulses per second, while 90 percent of your unconscious brain processes 40 million nerve impulses per second (6). That means we are ruled by our subconscious behaviors unless we do something about it. Journaling is one of the most effective ways to pause and take inventory of what goes on in our own heads, helping to surface insights that may not have happened otherwise.

Now that you know the benefits, here are three important ground rules, or reminders, I invite you to remember:

1) **You are limitless!** How easily we can forget that. This is because around 90% of our brains are unconscious or in the subconscious, which means we don't realize we are limitless. It's like the analogy that each of us can live life like a goldfish in a fishbowl. If we don't challenge ourselves to go outside of what we know, we don't realize or experience the life that's possible beyond the fishbowl. We're governed by our belief systems (which were shaped most likely before the age of seven in our families), where we grew up, and how we grew up. As adults, we have a duty to shift those beliefs so that we can reach our potential. That's what creating your dreams is all about, right?

2) **Dig deep and be a truth teller.** Be courageous to share vulnerably and honestly about how you feel, your challenges, and fears — along with all the things you desire and celebrate. If you have a crappy day, write about it instead of avoiding the painful topic. This will help you move through and beyond your blocks as you get real and honest with yourself. As we all know, "The truth will make you free" (7).

3) **Write as if your dreams depended on it.** They kind of do. 'Nuff said!

Chapter 2

How to Maximize

Intentional Writing

Excellence is never an accident. It is always the result of high intention, sincere effort, and intelligent execution; it represents the wise choice of many alternatives. Choice, not chance, determines your destiny. — Aristotle

Ok, now let's get down to intentional pausing...aka journal business. How does journaling help you create your dreams? Well, it's all about intention. That's why I've selected specific daily writing prompts to guide you.

The word "intention" stems from the 14th Century Old French *entencion* or "aspiration," and the Latin word *intendio* meaning, "stretching or purpose" (1). Today Merriam-Webster defines it as, "The thing you plan to do or achieve" (2). In medical terms, healing by "first intention" is the process of the healing of wound (3). As my mentor Dr. Bob Wright would remind me, intention is aliveness with direction (4). All of these definitions (especially that medical one) remind us of the personal power we are capable of when we bring our intention to something we do. In intentional writing, we fire off our flare guns to our brain signaling, "Hey, pay attention — this matters!"

In order to move forward toward what we want to accomplish and achieve, whether it's our dreams or our plans for the day, it is essential to have intention. This requires us be aware of where we are at and how we feel. We need to acknowledge and understand our own history to glean the lessons from it. In journaling, this rule applies. When we write down how we feel or where we are at, we can then set a course for where we want to go, which can either be how we want to feel, or a dream we desire to fulfill. In *Pause: The Journal*, we can do this in a single entry. This might include the healing process of a wound or an aspiration, as you give it attention, time, or words. It might include having a word of the day reminding yourself of where you want to go. It means getting off of autopilot and bringing your conscious mind to your journal practice.

———————

Pro tip: Vision can be even more powerful than goals because it's our north star for where we want to go as we accomplish our goals! If you are not setting a vision for where you want to go (also known as *your dreams*), how can you expect to get there? Our minds and hearts need to have tools or "scaffolding," like seeing words on paper and picturing something in progress. When our minds can grasp something tangible, we're much more likely to obtain it. Research tells us even by writing down what your goals are, you are 42% more likely to obtain them (5).

Remember, when writing with the intention to express thoughts, processing what is top of mind and simply brain dumping can be a powerful and effective way to move through any challenge or block that is keeping us from our ideal outcomes. What's important to consider, and not always that obvious when writing, is that journaling isn't only a tool for processing, but a tool for creating what we want more of in our lives. Call it manifesting, creating, or harnessing your long-term vision and goals — they don't just happen. We need to believe we can make it happen and be intentional about generating what we truly desire in our lives.

That's what *Pause: The Journal* is all about. It's not just writing to process the past or contemplate the present, although those are important steps to support you on your journey. *Pause: The Journal* is about creating the future through intentional writing.

Here's a few more pro tips for how to maximize this journal in service to your dreams.

1) **Start Where You Are.** Take a few conscious breaths before you write. Ground yourself in the date and time and say it aloud. Add your personal fuel tank rating for the day, or how much energy you have, and select a word of the day and heading to orient yourself. Celebrate something good that happened yesterday so your hippocampus is primed for creativity. Now that's intentional!

2) **Spend two minutes writing in your stream of consciousness.** Use the blank slate page to capture thoughts or images and what is top of mind as you write. Set a timer for two minutes and stop after two minutes. When we empty out our brains (and ideally suspend judgement as we do so), we can feel calmer and clearer, and be less in our monkey-mind chatter. We can also come to new insights or *aha*'s as a result.

Now, let's cover the individual prompts and what they mean.

Chapter 3

How to Use This Journal: Follow the Prompts

Being aware is more important than being smart.
— Phil Jackson

- **Read the daily quote.** Each entry begins with an inspiration. That's how every day should be, right? Allow this quote to sink in, or maybe incorporate it in your writing prompts or on your blank slate second page.
- **Write today's date and take a few conscious breaths.** Take a moment to ground yourself. Connect with your breath for three or more conscious breaths. Write and speak the date to yourself. The point is to center yourself and feel connected to your body before you begin.
- **Personal Fuel Tank Rating 1-10.** Check in with your current energy level. Consider physical, mental, and

emotional energy. Give yourself a rating from 1 (lowest energy) to 10 (highest energy). Depending on your rating, you can navigate your day feeling equipped on how to resource yourself.

- **Word of the day (WoD) or headline.** What is your intentional word(s) to orient to today? Your "WoD" serves as a signal for what your day is about and how to make your day purposeful. Some examples are: aliveness, playful, or in flow. You can take this one step further and imagine your day has a headline. If you were reading the news about what your day was like, what would it be? Have fun with it. "Kathryn knows she matters," or "Salsa dancing starts today!" are examples.

- **Today I desire.** What do you truly desire *today*? Much more on this in the last chapter, but what you desire can be your "why" behind your word or headline. This can also include the 1-3 things that you want to accomplish or prioritize. Is it to feel connected? To feel alive? To finish your proposal? To attend a yoga class? When we anchor our dreams to what we desire and our intentional actions, we can feel more aligned with what we're going after, get clearer on what we want to accomplish, and be more purposeful.

———

Pro Tip: Celebrate what you did desire (to do or what desires were met) the next day when you write down your celebrations!

———

- **Dream worth pausing for and why.** Using present tense, write down one of your dreams. If "dream" doesn't speak to you, swap in another word such as "goal", "accomplishment" or "what I want to create." Another way to think of this is, what successful outcome are you interested in creating and/or manifesting? Imagine that you've actually achieved this dream and allow yourself to feel.

Pro Tip 1: Use your five senses to tap into your dream. Close your eyes. How does your body feel? Are you smiling, or are you giggling? Who are you sharing your wonderful news with? Imagine feelings of excitement, joy, pride, celebration, and gratitude as you achieve this dream. If you notice fear, acknowledge that too. It is part of the process of going after your dreams. Excitement and fear feel the same in the body, so you can tell yourself, "I'm just excited," to help mitigate the fear. Anything you write down is you taking one step towards making it more real.

Pro Tip 2: Faking it 'til you make it can help here. Give yourself permission to think big and imagine something has already happened in your life that you accomplished. Have fun with it!

Pro Tip 3: It's important to remember your *why*. Ask yourself *why* does this dream matter? This can be your purpose behind doing it. The more you connect with your *why*, the more connected you will be to yourself and to achieving your dream. Write down why this dream matters or use the blank slate page to elaborate.

————————

- **One little thing to do today toward your dream.** What's one thing, one step, or one action you can take today toward your dream? It could be the next thing that gets you closer: sending an email, telling someone about your dream you haven't told yet, or reaching out to someone. Think of it like your inspired bias to action that will help you move toward your dream.
- **Vision for the day.** Think of this as your daily mantra. Who could you become? This is about yourself as you move through your day. Stick with using first person, present tense.

  - **Examples:** *I stay connected and focused. I am exactly where I need to be. I create my desires. I have fun while I engage with others.*
- **Celebrate & Gratitude.** When we celebrate something, we are accentuating the positive, or *pause-a-tive*, from something that happened that our brains may miss if we were on autopilot. To create your dreams, celebrating your

journey is a big part of the process to stay the course. Maybe you ate a healthy breakfast, exercised, found a good novel, or made time to journal. Another way to think of this is: *what's something good that has already happened to you?* You can also add in a few things you are grateful for right now.

Pro Tip: Don't think too hard about what you are grateful for. It can be something in general, or a crystallized moment you experienced. Is it the roof over your head? Is it the sun piercing through the window? Is it your cat curling up on your lap? Research tells us that gratitude is a gateway for feeling more joy, orienting toward the positive, and helps us dream of what's possible. That's what creating your dreams through intentional writing is all about. Gratitude, in a way, ties it all together.

- **Write yourself a mini support or "love" note.** This can be a sentence or two from your higher self, or wise self, who is sharing from your kind, supportive, encouraging self. If that feels challenging, imagine you were a wise, kind friend giving a few words of encouragement. If you are journaling as part of a group, it can also be a note of gratitude or support to someone and can be shared within the group.
  - **Example:** *Dear Ray, I love your work on your body reset. You are amazing!* (Written to self).

- o **Example:** *Chris, you rocked it! I am so proud of all that you are focused on right now. Keep going.* (Written to self).

- o **Example:** *John, I really liked the way you supported me last week in our group. Thank you for your kind words, you were so helpful.* (Written to a teammate in group journaling).

- **Blank Slate Page.** Use this page for anything that's on your mind or to expand on any of the prompts. It can be written or visual. Be intentional about what you want out of this page. Is it to process an event? Share an experience? Express how you feel? Brain dump? Express how you feel or what's going on? Anything goes. You're adding momentum for a desired outcome though images, poems, or prose on this page. Let your stream of consciousness flow.

––––––––––––

Pro Tip: Put on some music or sit in a place that feels comforting and replenishing for you. If you need more space to write, use the "notes and check-in" pages after the journal prompt pages.

––––––––––––

Chapter 4

Five Hacks for Optimizing

Pause: The Journal

Unless commitment is made, there are only promises and hopes; but no plans. — Peter Drucker

Many of us high-achiever types love to optimize! Here's my top hacks for how to get the most out of *Pause: The Journal*. This could go for anything you set your mind to —feel free to apply it in other areas in your life.

1. **Commit.** Incorporate journaling as a daily ritual or set regular time aside to focus on how you want to shift and take action to make it happen. Pick a time that works, like first thing when you get up, or before you go to bed, and put it in your calendar.

2. **Dedicate this journal as sacred space.** Trust in the process and what comes to mind as you write.

Allow the pen to flow without too much deliberating. Since you are the only one who will read your journal, write whatever comes up for you. This is a sacred process unfolding, and it's important to treat it as such. Honor what you write as where you are TODAY. Later on, you can re-read what is written, and reflect from there knowing this mattered for you when you wrote it.

3. **Breathe.** That's right, inhale through your nose, exhale through your mouth at a slower, relaxed pace for (at least) five deep breaths before you write. Count each breath starting with the first deep breath. If you get to ten, even better. This will help clear your mind before writing and allow thoughts to become clearer. Even if you're not sure what to write when you start, just taking the pen and writing down whatever comes to mind is great. That is what this journal is for: emptying your mind. That way, you can reflect from a clear perspective in a grounded, embodied state.

4. **Write in the present tense**. Capture how you feel and what you sense to stay in present time. Avoid diving into a story, as tempting as that is, as it has already happened and keeps us stuck in our limiting beliefs, drama, or patterns. What observations about yourself do you have on staying present?

5. **Have fun.** When we allow ourselves to be creative and playful as we step into more possibilities, we are much more likely to get there. If we are in doubt, then we are

much more likely to remain in negative thoughts or feel stuck. Our brains are wired for negativity and keeping us safe. We also resist change. Reaching our dreams invites us to step out of our comfort zones. It is way easier to do when we keep our sense of humor. One of the easiest ways I know how to do that is to write, including mini "love notes" to ourselves as we stay positive, encouraging, and playful.

Bonus Tip: Write down first impressions, gut reactions, questions you have, and ideas you create. All are wonderful expressions of yourself, and you don't have to share it with anyone. Don't worry about finding the right words or expressing yourself in a good light. Trust in the journaling process.

Practical tips to keep in mind:

- Don't worry about punctuation or spelling. Write quickly and give yourself permission for your thoughts and emotions to flow.
- Use the same journal and pen daily. I invite you to dedicate your writing utensil to your practice.
- Dedicating the same time each day to journaling is also a plus: it creates a consistent structure and routine to adhere to.

- You don't need to write every day. Be intentional about it (e.g. *I will write five days a week, or on weekends.*).

- Keep your journal private. This is your safe space to work through potentially distressing or confusing thoughts and emotions. If you're writing as part of a team or group effort, you can share about *how* the experience is, challenges you have, or wins from the journaling process. More on this in the next chapter about how to use *Pause: The Journal* with a group of people.

Chapter 5

Leverage

Pause: The Journal

in a Group or Team

A dream you dream alone is only a dream. A dream you dream together is reality. — John Lennon

We all know the power of one person's intentional writing, but what if an entire team or group used intentional writing to amplify a shared vision or dream? Or, used intentional writing as a way to build trust and rapport as a community focused on one initiative? What if a group used gratitude prompts or love notes (also known as *thank you notes*) to express appreciation? After all, gratitude can increase productivity in the workplace 50% by saying a simple "thank you" (1).

Read on, team player! *Pause: The Journal* is great for every type of community. You can use this journal for improving performance, morale, productivity, and creativity. From executive leadership to sports teams, members of any community can intentionally write in service to reaching your shared vision, dreams, or goals.

How to Use *Pause: The Journal* for Group Intentional Writing

- **Have Two Visions.** If you lead a team using *Pause: The Journal*, create a vision for yourself AND your group's desired outcome. Each person can do the same: one vision for themselves, and one vision for the group outcome... Is your dream to launch a new product? To find your soul mate? To have fun and connect? To discover what dreams you may have as individuals? It can be anything.

  ○ For each vision, use the present tense, first person. It should feel out of your comfort zone and also something you could orient to at any given time. So it's not about an out-there, lofty goal. Rather, it's about what you want to do moment by moment as you orient toward the vision you want to create.

- Discuss weekly, or even daily, how the journaling is going as a group. You can get into groups of two or three people and discuss how you show up, what impact you want to have, and what you are experiencing or feeling as a result of intentional writing. This helps support the group in a holistic way. It can also feel motivating, supportive, and unifying.

• Even though you are focusing on a specific vision from the group, bring your whole self to the journal. Direct your thoughts and writing toward the group's shared intention. You can acknowledge your personal hopes and fears. When you acknowledge where you are, it may be easier to identify new ways of thinking and solutions that can be helpful.

Fill out this section before you begin as a group:
   Name of group:
   Who is invited to journal:

   Why are we journaling as a group?

   Vision for myself:

   Vision for our group/team:

   Duration to Journal:
   ☐ **One Week**
   ☐ **Two Weeks**
   ☐ **Thirty Days**
   ☐ **Sixty Days**
   ☐ **Ninety Days**
   ☐ **Custom:**

   Additional thoughts, notes or comments:

Pro Tip for Creating Your Individual and Group Vision

One variation while writing as a group is to have a collective vision or desired outcome, along with your individual vision. You can come up with this as a group together. Here are some examples of what that could look like below. As part of the group discussion process, you can choose to share individual visions as part of a group. It's an opportunity to be inspired, provide helpful feedback, and be accountable! (Recall we are 42% more likely to reach our goals when we write them down and tell others about them!)

Scenario A: An executive leadership team is striving to hit $5 million US dollars in revenue this quarter for the first time. An individual vision could be, "I show up and do what it takes as a resourced and talented contributor." The group vision everyone accepts, perhaps after agreeing to this upon discussion would be, "Our team supports each other with bias to action as we make our $5M target this quarter."

Scenario B: A community of women business leaders use *Pause: The Journal* for 30 days to journal on and create what they are focused on in life. One woman wants to launch her dream business. One wants a career change. One wants to spend more time with her kids. Each journaler would have an individual vision, such as "I take action every day to build my business," or "I am open and research my career options every day," or "I spend quality time with my children." However, the group vision could be, "We support each other as we move towards our individual desires."

———————————

Additional Hacks for High-Achieving Groups and Individuals

What gets in the way when it comes to reaching a shared dream or vision? Sometimes, it is the drive of the relentless perfectionist, striving to get it right. We want to get it perfect, and as a result, we don't move forward. We fear judgement (from ourselves or others) that we are not good enough. One hack my clients learn is to embrace the mantra, "It's not about perfection, it's about completion." Intentional writing is about completion, even if it's for thirty seconds that day. Here's a few things to keep in mind as you focus as a group.

•   **Follow *Pause: The Journal* guidelines first as an individual.** As a group, the only difference is to use the lens of whatever your group or team is oriented toward. What are you looking to achieve together? What is the desired outcome? If you're looking to launch a product, the lens zooms in on this topic for your entry. Maybe you are looking to enjoy the process of writing in and of itself, as a group. Maybe you're starting your own journal club and the individuals in your group have separate, unique dreams or desires to create. As you journal, write from your perspective.

•   **Keep the focus on what your group's initiative is.** It may be the corporate world, a book club, a non-profit, an educational cohort, a journaling club, or a group focused on career changes/transition, money, relationships, or family. Anything goes! You can keep the focus open to what you decide as a group.

- **Periodically share highlights (and lowlights) about what it's like to intentionally write.** Check in and ask others how it is going. It doesn't mean you need to share what you specifically wrote, but rather the experience of journaling. You may notice themes or challenges the group experiences collectively. Discussing these is a great way to overcome any challenges, gel together as a team, and learn more about each other. Maybe you describe how you feel, or share how you show up, who you partner with, or who are your allies are. Use the free-form blank slate page to flush this out. This is a great way for any group to collaborate and support each other, even if the focus is journaling as an individual while in a group.

Now that you know how to leverage *Pause: The Journal* for a group, it's time to learn more about how to 10x your results and deliver on your dreams in our next chapter.

Chapter 6

How to 10x Your Dreams: Anchor Your Dreams with Your Yearnings

Keep your eyes on the stars, and your feet on the ground.
— Theodore Roosevelt

It's powerful to write down your intentions, but it can be ten times more powerful when they are connected to what truly matters to you. These are called your deeper desires or yearnings. Here's a step-by-step guide on where to start.

1) Before you write, notice your deeper desires, or yearnings.

In their book *Heart of the Fight: A Couple's Guide to Fifteen Common Fights, What They Really Mean, and How They Can Bring You Closer*, Drs. Bob and Judith Wright define yearnings as "adaptive mechanisms that initially developed for our survival" (1). That means all 8 billion of us on the planet are hard-wired to yearn. We *are* our desires. This is what drives us to relate, to bond, and to commune with others as well as to develop ourselves. Do you want to be safe? Or be seen? Do you yearn to be loved or to matter? Do you yearn to make a difference? These are a few universal hungers, or yearnings.

As I note in the book *Pause: Harnessing the Life Changing Power of Giving Yourself a Break*, as humans, we are designed to yearn, and it happens throughout our lifetime (2). Evolution rewards us when we follow our yearnings with a flood to our system of feel-good neurochemicals (3). Your emotions are directly connected to your yearnings. The more you are in tune with how you feel, the more capable you are to express your emotions and fulfill your yearnings. How many times have you wanted to say (or journal) something or share how you feel, but decided it wasn't worth it, or didn't follow through? Every time you decide it's not worth it, you are, on some level, saying *you* aren't worth it.

When we do not fulfill our yearnings, they surface in other ways, like checking social media every chance we get and feeling connected through technology. If you learn to discern surface wants (*Let me check my email*) from deeper yearnings (*I want a hug*) in any given moment, you can focus on fulfilling your underlying yearning and feel more satisfied (4). Our surface level actions indicate deeper yearnings we all have.

When we can connect our dreams to our deeper desires or yearnings, it's as if we are anchoring valid, concrete evidence why they are so important to us. They are no longer whimsical or lofty, but aligned with what truly is desired. Our priorities and actions can also align to fulfill our yearnings. We can become even more committed, motivated, and inspired. Our dreams resonate at a deeper level within us because we can feel and connect with them not just as words on paper, but as an extension of our being and doing.

Go the extra mile. Pause to identify your yearnings as you write. It is a powerful way to align your surface level thoughts, or what you are looking to create, with your deeper-rooted yearnings. In each entry, you can pause and identify your yearnings, or desires, as a check-in to align with what really matters. Yearning to make a difference? Is your dream representing this? When you anchor your dreams to what you yearn for, your dreams are that much more potent and powerful. They are more enriched in your authentic you! You are connected in mind, body, and soul, and this will translate to even more intentional and meaningful dreams.

Sometimes, it is difficult to identify what we yearn for if all we see, think, or write about is on the surface. Pausing to journal is one way to raise your awareness and align with what matters.

Here's a few examples of yearnings. *What do you yearn for?* What a great topic for a journal entry.

- To feel alive (to experience fully, to create, to express, to learn, and grow)
- To be secure (to exist, to connect, to trust)
- To be loved (to love, to feel appreciated, to belong, to connect)
- To matter (to be valued, to contribute, to make a difference)

2. Separate your yearnings from your surface-level wants.

Sometimes, it is difficult to identify what we yearn for if all we see or think about is on the surface. Pausing is one way you can raise your awareness and align with what your deeper yearnings are. If you're in need of an intervention, chances are you may be off track. A great way to uncover yearnings is to employ what Drs. Wright call the "so that" test (5).

Think of something that you want, like vacation (or a pause). If you apply the "I want X so that..." format to this desire, you can uncover a new layer.

I want a vacation...*so that* I can feel less stress

I want to feel less stress *so that* I can relax and snorkel at the beach.

I want to snorkel at the beach *so that* I experience the thrill.

I want to feel the thrill of snorkeling *so that* I can feel alive.

I want to feel alive...I yearn to feel alive...

What do you yearn for? Is there a surface "want" to placate your deeper yearning(s)?

Does your dream help you meet your yearning? When we become aware of what we yearn for, our dreams can become even more significant. On the flipside, any dreams that aren't aligned with our deeper yearnings may fade away, leaving room for new dreams to emerge that feel more aligned and purposeful.

Now, let's create some intentional writing in service to your vision, and your dreams.

Let the adventure begin.

Journal

The wisdom is in the pause. — Alice Walker

Date:_____ Personal Fuel Tank Rating (1-10): _____

Word(s) of the day or headline:

_____

_____

Today I desire:

_____

_____

Dream worth pausing for:

_____

_____

One little thing I can do today towards it:

_____

_____

Vision for the day:

_____

_____

_____

Celebration & gratitude pause:

_____

_____

_____

Support note to myself:

_____

_____

_____

Blank Slate Page:

May the force be with you until you know you are the force.
— R. Buckminster Fuller

Date:_____ Personal Fuel Tank Rating (1-10): _____

Word(s) of the day or headline:

_____

_____

Today I desire:

_____

_____

Dream worth pausing for:

_____

_____

One little thing I can do today towards it:

_____

_____

Vision for the day:

_____

_____

_____

Celebration & gratitude pause:

_____

_____

_____

Support note to myself:

_____

_____

_____

Blank Slate Page:

You are the master of your destiny. You can influence, direct, and control your own environment. You can make your life what you want it to be. — Napoleon Hill

Date:_____ Personal Fuel Tank Rating (1-10): _____

Word(s) of the day or headline:

_____

_____

Today I desire:

_____

_____

Dream worth pausing for:

_____

_____

One little thing I can do today towards it:

_____

_____

Vision for the day:

_____

_____

_____

Celebration & gratitude pause:

_____

_____

_____

Support note to myself:

_____

_____

Blank Slate Page:

Strengthen your hopes, not your fears. — Nelson Mandela

Date:_____ Personal Fuel Tank Rating (1-10): _____

Word(s) of the day or headline:

_____

_____

Today I desire:

_____

_____

Dream worth pausing for:

_____

_____

One little thing I can do today towards it:

_____

_____

Vision for the day:

_____

_____

_____

Celebration & gratitude pause:

_____

_____

_____

Support note to myself:

_____

_____

_____

Blank Slate Page:

Between stimulus and response there is a space. In that space is the power to choose our response. In our response lies our growth and our freedom. — Viktor Frankl

Date:_____ Personal Fuel Tank Rating (1-10): _____

Word(s) of the day or headline:

_____

_____

Today I desire:

_____

_____

Dream worth pausing for:

_____

_____

One little thing I can do today towards it:

_____

_____

Vision for the day:

_____

_____

_____

Celebration & gratitude pause:

_____

_____

_____

Support note to myself:

_____

_____

Blank Slate Page:

The only dreams that come true are the ones you chase,
if you do nothing, you get nothing. — Joseph Atser

Date:_____ Personal Fuel Tank Rating (1-10): _____

Word(s) of the day or headline:

_____

_____

Today I desire:

_____

_____

Dream worth pausing for:

_____

_____

One little thing I can do today towards it:

_____

_____

Vision for the day:

_____

_____

_____

Celebration & gratitude pause:

_____

_____

_____

Support note to myself:

_____

_____

Blank Slate Page:

The purpose of childhood is formation. The purpose of adulthood is transformation. — Jack Mezirow

Date:_____ Personal Fuel Tank Rating (1-10): _____

Word(s) of the day or headline:

_____

_____

Today I desire:

_____

_____

Dream worth pausing for:

_____

_____

One little thing I can do today towards it:

_____

_____

Vision for the day:

_____

_____

_____

Celebration & gratitude pause:

_____

_____

_____

Support note to myself:

_____

_____

Blank Slate Page:

To be yourself in a world that is constantly trying to make you something else is the greatest accomplishment.
— Ralph Waldo Emerson

Date:_____ Personal Fuel Tank Rating (1-10): _____

Word(s) of the day or headline:

_____

_____

Today I desire:

_____

_____

Dream worth pausing for:

_____

_____

One little thing I can do today towards it:

_____

_____

Vision for the day:

_____

_____

_____

Celebration & gratitude pause:

_____

_____

_____

Support note to myself:

_____

_____

Blank Slate Page:

What is to give light must endure burning. — Victor Frankl

Date:_____ Personal Fuel Tank Rating (1-10): _____

Word(s) of the day or headline:

_____

_____

Today I desire:

_____

_____

Dream worth pausing for:

_____

_____

One little thing I can do today towards it:

_____

_____

Vision for the day:

_____

_____

_____

Celebration & gratitude pause:

_____

_____

_____

Support note to myself:

_____

_____

_____

Blank Slate Page:

Let everything happen to you. Beauty and terror. Just keep going. No feeling is final. — Rainer Maria Rilke

Date:_____ Personal Fuel Tank Rating (1-10): _____

Word(s) of the day or headline:

_____

_____

Today I desire:

_____

_____

Dream worth pausing for:

_____

_____

One little thing I can do today towards it:

_____

_____

Vision for the day:

_____

_____

_____

Celebration & gratitude pause:

_____

_____

_____

Support note to myself:

_____

_____

Blank Slate Page:

When you make the finding yourself — even if you're the last person on Earth to see the light — you'll never forget it.
— Carl Sagan

Date:_____ Personal Fuel Tank Rating (1-10): _____

Word(s) of the day or headline:

_____

_____

Today I desire:

_____

_____

Dream worth pausing for:

_____

_____

One little thing I can do today towards it:

_____

_____

Vision for the day:

_____

_____

_____

Celebration & gratitude pause:

_____

_____

_____

Support note to myself:

_____

_____

Blank Slate Page:

It is then that you will hear a voice within yourself. It was there all the time, but you never listened before.
— Rusty Berkus

Date:_____ Personal Fuel Tank Rating (1-10): _____

Word(s) of the day or headline:

_____

_____

Today I desire:

_____

_____

Dream worth pausing for:

_____

_____

One little thing I can do today towards it:

_____

_____

Vision for the day:

_____

_____

_____

Celebration & gratitude pause:

_____

_____

_____

Support note to myself:

_____

_____

Blank Slate Page:

A talent is found in stillness. — Goethe

Date:_____ Personal Fuel Tank Rating (1-10): _____

Word(s) of the day or headline:

_____

_____

Today I desire:

_____

_____

Dream worth pausing for:

_____

_____

One little thing I can do today towards it:

_____

_____

Vision for the day:

_____

_____

_____

Celebration & gratitude pause:

_____

_____

_____

Support note to myself:

_____

_____

_____

Blank Slate Page:

The minute you begin to do what you want to do, it's a different kind of life. — R. Buckminster Fuller

Date:_____ Personal Fuel Tank Rating (1-10): _____

Word(s) of the day or headline:

_____

_____

Today I desire:

_____

_____

Dream worth pausing for:

_____

_____

One little thing I can do today towards it:

_____

_____

Vision for the day:

_____

_____

_____

Celebration & gratitude pause:

_____

_____

_____

Support note to myself:

_____

_____

Blank Slate Page:

If you honor your inner voice your communication will come from a centered, grounded place. You are aligned and inspiring. — Rachael O'Meara

Date:_____ Personal Fuel Tank Rating (1-10): _____

Word(s) of the day or headline:

_____

_____

Today I desire:

_____

_____

Dream worth pausing for:

_____

_____

One little thing I can do today towards it:

_____

_____

Vision for the day:

_____

_____

_____

Celebration & gratitude pause:

_____

_____

_____

Support note to myself:

_____

_____

Blank Slate Page:

The only thing that will stop you from fulfilling your dreams is you. — Tom Bradley

Date:_____ Personal Fuel Tank Rating (1-10): _____

Word(s) of the day or headline:

_____

_____

Today I desire:

_____

_____

Dream worth pausing for:

_____

_____

One little thing I can do today towards it:

_____

_____

Vision for the day:

_____

_____

_____

Celebration & gratitude pause:

_____

_____

_____

Support note to myself:

_____

_____

Blank Slate Page:

Hope lies in dreams, in imagination, and in the courage of those who dare to make dreams into reality. — Jonas Salk

Date:_____ Personal Fuel Tank Rating (1-10): _____

Word(s) of the day or headline:

_____

_____

Today I desire:

_____

_____

Dream worth pausing for:

_____

_____

One little thing I can do today towards it:

_____

_____

Vision for the day:

_____

_____

_____

Celebration & gratitude pause:

_____

_____

_____

Support note to myself:

_____

_____

Blank Slate Page:

The very act of resting is the hardest and most courageous act once can perform. — Thomas Merton

Date:_____ Personal Fuel Tank Rating (1-10): _____

Word(s) of the day or headline:

_____

_____

Today I desire:

_____

_____

Dream worth pausing for:

_____

_____

One little thing I can do today towards it:

_____

_____

Vision for the day:

_____

_____

_____

Celebration & gratitude pause:

_____

_____

_____

Support note to myself:

_____

_____

_____

Blank Slate Page:

You are the master of your destiny. You can influence, direct, and control your own environment. You can make your life what you want it to be. — Napoleon Hill

Date:_____ Personal Fuel Tank Rating (1-10): _____

Word(s) of the day or headline:

_____

_____

Today I desire:

_____

_____

Dream worth pausing for:

_____

_____

One little thing I can do today towards it:

_____

_____

Vision for the day:

_____

_____

_____

Celebration & gratitude pause:

_____

_____

_____

Support note to myself:

_____

_____

Blank Slate Page:

Life is no 'brief candle' — it is a sort of splendid torch and I
want to make it burn as brightly as possible.
— George Bernard Shaw

Date:_____ Personal Fuel Tank Rating (1-10): _____

Word(s) of the day or headline:

_____

_____

Today I desire:

_____

_____

Dream worth pausing for:

_____

_____

One little thing I can do today towards it:

_____

_____

Vision for the day:

_____

_____

_____

Celebration & gratitude pause:

_____

_____

_____

Support note to myself:

_____

_____

Blank Slate Page:

He who can no longer pause to wonder and stand rapt in awe, is as good as dead; his eyes are closed.
— Albert Einstein

Date:_____ Personal Fuel Tank Rating (1-10): _____

Word(s) of the day or headline:

_____

_____

Today I desire:

_____

_____

Dream worth pausing for:

_____

_____

One little thing I can do today towards it:

_____

_____

Vision for the day:

_____

_____

_____

Celebration & gratitude pause:

_____

_____

_____

Support note to myself:

_____

_____

Blank Slate Page:

The inner voice can be very scary sometimes. You listen and then you go "do shut? I don't wanna do that!" But you still have to pay attention to it. — Alice Walker

Date:_____ Personal Fuel Tank Rating (1-10): _____

Word(s) of the day or headline:

_____

_____

Today I desire:

_____

_____

Dream worth pausing for:

_____

_____

One little thing I can do today towards it:

_____

_____

Vision for the day:

_____

_____

_____

Celebration & gratitude pause:

_____

_____

_____

Support note to myself:

_____

_____

Blank Slate Page:

Deep listening is when your inner voice emerges and is heard. It is too easy to miss it without a pause.
— Rachael O'Meara

Date:_____ Personal Fuel Tank Rating (1-10): _____

Word(s) of the day or headline:

_____

_____

Today I desire:

_____

_____

Dream worth pausing for:

_____

_____

One little thing I can do today towards it:

_____

_____

Vision for the day:

_____

_____

_____

Celebration & gratitude pause:

_____

_____

_____

Support note to myself:

_____

_____

Blank Slate Page:

Life was meant to be lived, and curiosity must be kept alive.
One must never, for whatever reason, turn his back on life.
— Eleanor Roosevelt

Date:_____ Personal Fuel Tank Rating (1-10): _____

Word(s) of the day or headline:

_____

_____

Today I desire:

_____

_____

Dream worth pausing for:

_____

_____

One little thing I can do today towards it:

_____

_____

Vision for the day:

_____

_____

_____

Celebration & gratitude pause:

_____

_____

_____

Support note to myself:

_____

_____

Blank Slate Page:

What lies behind us, and what lies before us are tiny matters, compared to what lies within us.
— Ralph Waldo Emerson

Date:_____ Personal Fuel Tank Rating (1-10): _____

Word(s) of the day or headline:

_____

_____

Today I desire:

_____

_____

Dream worth pausing for:

_____

_____

One little thing I can do today towards it:

_____

_____

Vision for the day:

_____

_____

_____

Celebration & gratitude pause:

_____

_____

_____

Support note to myself:

_____

_____

Blank Slate Page:

Human freedom involves our capacity to pause between the stimulus and response and in that pause, to choose the one response...to throw our weight. — Rollo May

Date:_____ Personal Fuel Tank Rating (1-10): _____

Word(s) of the day or headline:

_____

_____

Today I desire:

_____

_____

Dream worth pausing for:

_____

_____

One little thing I can do today towards it:

_____

_____

Vision for the day:

_____

_____

_____

Celebration & gratitude pause:

_____

_____

_____

Support note to myself:

_____

_____

Blank Slate Page:

Intention is one of the most powerful forces there is. What you mean when you do a thing will always determine the outcome. The law creates the world. — Brenna Yovanoff

Date:_____ Personal Fuel Tank Rating (1-10): _____

Word(s) of the day or headline:

_____

_____

Today I desire:

_____

_____

Dream worth pausing for:

_____

_____

One little thing I can do today towards it:

_____

_____

Vision for the day:

_____

_____

_____

Celebration & gratitude pause:

_____

_____

_____

Support note to myself:

_____

_____

Blank Slate Page:

The mind acts like an enemy for those who don't control it.
— The Bhagavad Gita

Date:_____ Personal Fuel Tank Rating (1-10): _____

Word(s) of the day or headline:

_____

_____

Today I desire:

_____

_____

Dream worth pausing for:

_____

_____

One little thing I can do today towards it:

_____

_____

Vision for the day:

_____

_____

_____

Celebration & gratitude pause:

_____

_____

_____

Support note to myself:

_____

_____

Blank Slate Page:

You become a human doing, not a human being.
— John Bradshaw

Date:_____ Personal Fuel Tank Rating (1-10): _____

Word(s) of the day or headline:

_____

_____

Today I desire:

_____

_____

Dream worth pausing for:

_____

_____

One little thing I can do today towards it:

_____

_____

Vision for the day:

_____

_____

_____

Celebration & gratitude pause:

_____

_____

_____

Support note to myself:

_____

_____

Blank Slate Page:

When we don't allow ourselves to feel our emotions... we create a dangerous situation for our mental, emotional and physical health. — Tabby Biddle

Date:_____ Personal Fuel Tank Rating (1-10): _____

Word(s) of the day or headline:

_____

_____

Today I desire:

_____

_____

Dream worth pausing for:

_____

_____

One little thing I can do today towards it:

_____

_____

Vision for the day:

_____

_____

_____

Celebration & gratitude pause:

_____

_____

_____

Support note to myself:

_____

_____

Blank Slate Page:

The definition of insanity is doing the same thing over and over and expecting different results. — Benjamin Franklin

Date:_____ Personal Fuel Tank Rating (1-10): _____

Word(s) of the day or headline:

_____

_____

Today I desire:

_____

_____

Dream worth pausing for:

_____

_____

One little thing I can do today towards it:

_____

_____

Vision for the day:

_____

_____

_____

Celebration & gratitude pause:

_____

_____

_____

Support note to myself:

_____

_____

Blank Slate Page:

Beware the banality of a busy life. — Socrates

Date:_____ Personal Fuel Tank Rating (1-10): _____

Word(s) of the day or headline:

_____

_____

Today I desire:

_____

_____

Dream worth pausing for:

_____

_____

One little thing I can do today towards it:

_____

_____

Vision for the day:

_____

_____

_____

Celebration & gratitude pause:

_____

_____

_____

Support note to myself:

_____

_____

_____

Blank Slate Page:

Consistent action creates consistent results.
— Christine Kane

Date:_____ Personal Fuel Tank Rating (1-10): _____

Word(s) of the day or headline:

_____

_____

Today I desire:

_____

_____

Dream worth pausing for:

_____

_____

One little thing I can do today towards it:

_____

_____

Vision for the day:

_____

_____

_____

Celebration & gratitude pause:

_____

_____

_____

Support note to myself:

_____

_____

Blank Slate Page:

A goal is a dream with a deadline. — Napoleon Hill

Date:_____ Personal Fuel Tank Rating (1-10): _____

Word(s) of the day or headline:

_____

_____

Today I desire:

_____

_____

Dream worth pausing for:

_____

_____

One little thing I can do today towards it:

_____

_____

Vision for the day:

_____

_____

_____

Celebration & gratitude pause:

_____

_____

_____

Support note to myself:

_____

_____

_____

Blank Slate Page:

Without strategy, execution is aimless. Without execution, strategy is useless. — Morris Chang

Date:_____ Personal Fuel Tank Rating (1-10): _____

Word(s) of the day or headline:

_____

_____

Today I desire:

_____

_____

Dream worth pausing for:

_____

_____

One little thing I can do today towards it:

_____

_____

Vision for the day:

_____

_____

_____

Celebration & gratitude pause:

_____

_____

_____

Support note to myself:

_____

_____

Blank Slate Page:

Whether you think you can, or you think you can't
— you're right. — Henry Ford

Date:_____ Personal Fuel Tank Rating (1-10): _____

Word(s) of the day or headline:

_____

_____

Today I desire:

_____

_____

Dream worth pausing for:

_____

_____

One little thing I can do today towards it:

_____

_____

Vision for the day:

_____

_____

_____

Celebration & gratitude pause:

_____

_____

_____

Support note to myself:

_____

_____

Blank Slate Page:

Be thankful for what you have; you'll end up having more. If you concentrate on what you don't have, you will never, ever have enough. — Oprah Winfrey

Date:_____ Personal Fuel Tank Rating (1-10): _____

Word(s) of the day or headline:

_____

_____

Today I desire:

_____

_____

Dream worth pausing for:

_____

_____

One little thing I can do today towards it:

_____

_____

Vision for the day:

_____

_____

_____

Celebration & gratitude pause:

_____

_____

_____

Support note to myself:

_____

_____

Blank Slate Page:

Don't underestimate the value of doing nothing, of just going along, listening to all the things you can't hear, and not bothering. — Winne the Pooh

Date:_____ Personal Fuel Tank Rating (1-10): _____

Word(s) of the day or headline:

_____

_____

Today I desire:

_____

_____

Dream worth pausing for:

_____

_____

One little thing I can do today towards it:

_____

_____

Vision for the day:

_____

_____

_____

Celebration & gratitude pause:

_____

_____

_____

Support note to myself:

_____

_____

Blank Slate Page:

*Healing can occur when we allow ourselves to feel, express,
and release emotions that we have suppressed.*
— Tabby Biddle

Date:_____ Personal Fuel Tank Rating (1-10): _____

Word(s) of the day or headline:

_____

_____

Today I desire:

_____

_____

Dream worth pausing for:

_____

_____

One little thing I can do today towards it:

_____

_____

Vision for the day:

_____

_____

_____

Celebration & gratitude pause:

_____

_____

_____

Support note to myself:

_____

_____

Blank Slate Page:

A pause is any intentional shift in behavior.
— Rachael O'Meara

Date:_____ Personal Fuel Tank Rating (1-10): _____

Word(s) of the day or headline:

_____

_____

Today I desire:

_____

_____

Dream worth pausing for:

_____

_____

One little thing I can do today towards it:

_____

_____

Vision for the day:

_____

_____

_____

Celebration & gratitude pause:

_____

_____

_____

Support note to myself:

_____

_____

Blank Slate Page:

This is the real secret of life — to be completely engaged with what you are doing in the here and now. — Alan Watts

Date:_____ Personal Fuel Tank Rating (1-10): _____

Word(s) of the day or headline:

_____

_____

Today I desire:

_____

_____

Dream worth pausing for:

_____

_____

One little thing I can do today towards it:

_____

_____

Vision for the day:

_____

_____

_____

Celebration & gratitude pause:

_____

_____

_____

Support note to myself:

_____

_____

Blank Slate Page:

Be here now. — Ram Dass

Date:_____ Personal Fuel Tank Rating (1-10): _____

Word(s) of the day or headline:

_____

_____

Today I desire:

_____

_____

Dream worth pausing for:

_____

_____

One little thing I can do today towards it:

_____

_____

Vision for the day:

_____

_____

_____

Celebration & gratitude pause:

_____

_____

_____

Support note to myself:

_____

_____

_____

Blank Slate Page:

We must be willing to get rid of the life we've planned, so as to have the life that is waiting for us. — Joseph Campbell

Date:_____ Personal Fuel Tank Rating (1-10): _____

Word(s) of the day or headline:

_____

_____

Today I desire:

_____

_____

Dream worth pausing for:

_____

_____

One little thing I can do today towards it:

_____

_____

Vision for the day:

_____

_____

_____

Celebration & gratitude pause:

_____

_____

_____

Support note to myself:

_____

_____

Blank Slate Page:

How wonderful it is that nobody need wait a single moment before starting to improve the world. — Anne Frank

Date:_____ Personal Fuel Tank Rating (1-10): _____

Word(s) of the day or headline:

_____

_____

Today I desire:

_____

_____

Dream worth pausing for:

_____

_____

One little thing I can do today towards it:

_____

_____

Vision for the day:

_____

_____

_____

Celebration & gratitude pause:

_____

_____

_____

Support note to myself:

_____

_____

Blank Slate Page:

A dream is just a dream. A goal is a dream with a plan and a deadline. — Harvey Mackay

Date:_____ Personal Fuel Tank Rating (1-10): _____

Word(s) of the day or headline:

_____

_____

Today I desire:

_____

_____

Dream worth pausing for:

_____

_____

One little thing I can do today towards it:

_____

_____

Vision for the day:

_____

_____

_____

Celebration & gratitude pause:

_____

_____

_____

Support note to myself:

_____

_____

Blank Slate Page:

Sometimes you need to press pause to let everything sink in.
— Sebastian Vettel

Date:_____ Personal Fuel Tank Rating (1-10): _____

Word(s) of the day or headline:

_____

_____

Today I desire:

_____

_____

Dream worth pausing for:

_____

_____

One little thing I can do today towards it:

_____

_____

Vision for the day:

_____

_____

_____

Celebration & gratitude pause:

_____

_____

_____

Support note to myself:

_____

_____

Blank Slate Page:

As human beings, our greatness lies not so much in being able to remake the world... as in being able to remake ourselves. — Mahatma Gandhi

Date:_____ Personal Fuel Tank Rating (1-10): _____

Word(s) of the day or headline:

_____

_____

Today I desire:

_____

_____

Dream worth pausing for:

_____

_____

One little thing I can do today towards it:

_____

_____

Vision for the day:

_____

_____

_____

Celebration & gratitude pause:

_____

_____

_____

Support note to myself:

_____

_____

Blank Slate Page:

Honesty is the first chapter of the book of wisdom.
— Thomas Jefferson

Date:_____ Personal Fuel Tank Rating (1-10): _____

Word(s) of the day or headline:

_____

_____

Today I desire:

_____

_____

Dream worth pausing for:

_____

_____

One little thing I can do today towards it:

_____

_____

Vision for the day:

_____

_____

_____

Celebration & gratitude pause:

_____

_____

_____

Support note to myself:

_____

_____

Blank Slate Page:

The principle of art is to pause, not bypass. — Jerzy Kosinski

Date:_____ Personal Fuel Tank Rating (1-10): _____

Word(s) of the day or headline:

_____

_____

Today I desire:

_____

_____

Dream worth pausing for:

_____

_____

One little thing I can do today towards it:

_____

_____

Vision for the day:

_____

_____

_____

Celebration & gratitude pause:

_____

_____

_____

Support note to myself:

_____

_____

_____

Blank Slate Page:

There comes a pause, for human strength will not endure to dance without cessation; and everyone must reach the point at length of absolute prostration. — Lewis Carroll

Date:_____ Personal Fuel Tank Rating (1-10): _____

Word(s) of the day or headline:

_____

_____

Today I desire:

_____

_____

Dream worth pausing for:

_____

_____

One little thing I can do today towards it:

_____

_____

Vision for the day:

_____

_____

_____

Celebration & gratitude pause:

_____

_____

_____

Support note to myself:

_____

_____

Blank Slate Page:

We are what we repeatedly do. — Aristotle

Date:_____ Personal Fuel Tank Rating (1-10): _____
Word(s) of the day or headline:

_____

_____

Today I desire:

_____

_____

Dream worth pausing for:

_____

_____

One little thing I can do today towards it:

_____

_____

Vision for the day:

_____

_____

_____

Celebration & gratitude pause:

_____

_____

_____

Support note to myself:

_____

_____

_____

Blank Slate Page:

Our intention creates our reality. — Wayne Dyer

Date:_____ Personal Fuel Tank Rating (1-10): _____

Word(s) of the day or headline:

_____

_____

Today I desire:

_____

_____

Dream worth pausing for:

_____

_____

One little thing I can do today towards it:

_____

_____

Vision for the day:

_____

_____

_____

Celebration & gratitude pause:

_____

_____

_____

Support note to myself:

_____

_____

_____

Blank Slate Page:

If your actions inspire others to dream more, learn more, do more, and become more, you are a leader.
— John Quincy Adams

Date:_____ Personal Fuel Tank Rating (1-10): _____

Word(s) of the day or headline:

_____

_____

Today I desire:

_____

_____

Dream worth pausing for:

_____

_____

One little thing I can do today towards it:

_____

_____

Vision for the day:

_____

_____

_____

Celebration & gratitude pause:

_____

_____

_____

Support note to myself:

_____

_____

Blank Slate Page:

To do the useful thing, to say the courageous thing, to contemplate the beautiful thing: that is enough for one man's life. — T.S. Eliot

Date:_____ Personal Fuel Tank Rating (1-10): _____

Word(s) of the day or headline:

_____

_____

Today I desire:

_____

_____

Dream worth pausing for:

_____

_____

One little thing I can do today towards it:

_____

_____

Vision for the day:

_____

_____

_____

Celebration & gratitude pause:

_____

_____

_____

Support note to myself:

_____

_____

Blank Slate Page:

'I'm afraid!' That proved that you find joy in living. It's normal to feel fear at certain moments. — Paulo Coelho

Date:_____ Personal Fuel Tank Rating (1-10): _____

Word(s) of the day or headline:

_____

_____

Today I desire:

_____

_____

Dream worth pausing for:

_____

_____

One little thing I can do today towards it:

_____

_____

Vision for the day:

_____

_____

_____

Celebration & gratitude pause:

_____

_____

_____

Support note to myself:

_____

_____

Blank Slate Page:

Change your thoughts and change the world.
— Norman Vincent Peale

Date:_____ Personal Fuel Tank Rating (1-10): _____

Word(s) of the day or headline:

_____

_____

Today I desire:

_____

_____

Dream worth pausing for:

_____

_____

One little thing I can do today towards it:

_____

_____

Vision for the day:

_____

_____

_____

Celebration & gratitude pause:

_____

_____

_____

Support note to myself:

_____

_____

Blank Slate Page:

We are our choices. — Jean-Paul Sartre

Date:_____ Personal Fuel Tank Rating (1-10): _____

Word(s) of the day or headline:

_____

_____

Today I desire:

_____

_____

Dream worth pausing for:

_____

_____

One little thing I can do today towards it:

_____

_____

Vision for the day:

_____

_____

_____

Celebration & gratitude pause:

_____

_____

_____

Support note to myself:

_____

_____

_____

Blank Slate Page:

You are the power of pause.
You always have the choice to pause. — Rachael O'Meara

Date:_____ Personal Fuel Tank Rating (1-10): _____
Word(s) of the day or headline:

_____

_____

Today I desire:

_____

_____

Dream worth pausing for:

_____

_____

One little thing I can do today towards it:

_____

_____

Vision for the day:

_____

_____

_____

Celebration & gratitude pause:

_____

_____

_____

Support note to myself:

_____

_____

Blank Slate Page:

Nothing happens unless first we dream. — Carl Sandburg

Date:_____ Personal Fuel Tank Rating (1-10): _____
Word(s) of the day or headline:

_____

_____

Today I desire:

_____

_____

Dream worth pausing for:

_____

_____

One little thing I can do today towards it:

_____

_____

Vision for the day:

_____

_____

_____

Celebration & gratitude pause:

_____

_____

_____

Support note to myself:

_____

_____

_____

Blank Slate Page:

*And the time came when the risk to remain tight in a bud
was more painful than the risk it took to blossom.*
— Anais Nin

Date:_____ Personal Fuel Tank Rating (1-10): _____

Word(s) of the day or headline:

_____

_____

Today I desire:

_____

_____

Dream worth pausing for:

_____

_____

One little thing I can do today towards it:

_____

_____

Vision for the day:

_____

_____

_____

Celebration & gratitude pause:

_____

_____

_____

Support note to myself:

_____

_____

Blank Slate Page:

Abundance is knowing that everything you need has already been supplied. — Shantidasa

Date:_____ Personal Fuel Tank Rating (1-10): _____

Word(s) of the day or headline:

_____

_____

Today I desire:

_____

_____

Dream worth pausing for:

_____

_____

One little thing I can do today towards it:

_____

_____

Vision for the day:

_____

_____

_____

Celebration & gratitude pause:

_____

_____

_____

Support note to myself:

_____

_____

Blank Slate Page:

The only limit to the height of your achievements is the reach of your dreams and the willingness to work hard for them. — Michelle Obama

Date:_____ Personal Fuel Tank Rating (1-10): _____

Word(s) of the day or headline:

_____

_____

Today I desire:

_____

_____

Dream worth pausing for:

_____

_____

One little thing I can do today towards it:

_____

_____

Vision for the day:

_____

_____

_____

Celebration & gratitude pause:

_____

_____

_____

Support note to myself:

_____

_____

Blank Slate Page:

You are never too old to set another goal
or to dream a new dream. — C.S. Lewis

Date:_____ Personal Fuel Tank Rating (1-10): _____

Word(s) of the day or headline:

_____

_____

Today I desire:

_____

_____

Dream worth pausing for:

_____

_____

One little thing I can do today towards it:

_____

_____

Vision for the day:

_____

_____

_____

Celebration & gratitude pause:

_____

_____

_____

Support note to myself:

_____

_____

Blank Slate Page:

No one has ever achieved anything from the smallest to the greatest unless the dream was dreamed first.
— Laura Ingalls Wilder

Date:_____ Personal Fuel Tank Rating (1-10): _____

Word(s) of the day or headline:

_____

_____

Today I desire:

_____

_____

Dream worth pausing for:

_____

_____

One little thing I can do today towards it:

_____

_____

Vision for the day:

_____

_____

_____

Celebration & gratitude pause:

_____

_____

_____

Support note to myself:

_____

_____

Blank Slate Page:

If you don't have a dream, how are you going to make a dream come true? — Oscar Hammerstein

Date:_____ Personal Fuel Tank Rating (1-10): _____

Word(s) of the day or headline:

_____

_____

Today I desire:

_____

_____

Dream worth pausing for:

_____

_____

One little thing I can do today towards it:

_____

_____

Vision for the day:

_____

_____

_____

Celebration & gratitude pause:

_____

_____

_____

Support note to myself:

_____

_____

Blank Slate Page:

And if not now, when? — The Talmund

Date:_____ Personal Fuel Tank Rating (1-10): _____
Word(s) of the day or headline:

_____

_____

Today I desire:

_____

_____

Dream worth pausing for:

_____

_____

One little thing I can do today towards it:

_____

_____

Vision for the day:

_____

_____

_____

Celebration & gratitude pause:

_____

_____

_____

Support note to myself:

_____

_____

_____

Blank Slate Page:

Only those who dare to fail greatly
can ever achieve greatly. — Robert F. Kennedy

Date:_____ Personal Fuel Tank Rating (1-10): _____

Word(s) of the day or headline:

_____

_____

Today I desire:

_____

_____

Dream worth pausing for:

_____

_____

One little thing I can do today towards it:

_____

_____

Vision for the day:

_____

_____

_____

Celebration & gratitude pause:

_____

_____

_____

Support note to myself:

_____

_____

Blank Slate Page:

If you can dream it, you can do it. — Walt Disney

Date:_____ Personal Fuel Tank Rating (1-10): _____

Word(s) of the day or headline:

_____

_____

Today I desire:

_____

_____

Dream worth pausing for:

_____

_____

One little thing I can do today towards it:

_____

_____

Vision for the day:

_____

_____

_____

Celebration & gratitude pause:

_____

_____

_____

Support note to myself:

_____

_____

_____

Blank Slate Page:

The future belongs to those who believe in the beauty of their dreams. — Eleanor Roosevelt

Date:_____ Personal Fuel Tank Rating (1-10): _____

Word(s) of the day or headline:

_____

_____

Today I desire:

_____

_____

Dream worth pausing for:

_____

_____

One little thing I can do today towards it:

_____

_____

Vision for the day:

_____

_____

_____

Celebration & gratitude pause:

_____

_____

_____

Support note to myself:

_____

_____

Blank Slate Page:

There are only two ways to live your life: one is as though nothing is a miracle; the other is as though everything is a miracle. — Albert Einstein

Date:_____ Personal Fuel Tank Rating (1-10): _____

Word(s) of the day or headline:

_____

_____

Today I desire:

_____

_____

Dream worth pausing for:

_____

_____

One little thing I can do today towards it:

_____

_____

Vision for the day:

_____

_____

_____

Celebration & gratitude pause:

_____

_____

_____

Support note to myself:

_____

_____

Blank Slate Page:

You don't have to be a fantastic hero to do certain things to compete. You can just an ordinary chap, sufficiently motivated to reach challenging goals. — Sir Edmund Hillary

Date:_____ Personal Fuel Tank Rating (1-10): _____

Word(s) of the day or headline:

_____

_____

Today I desire:

_____

_____

Dream worth pausing for:

_____

_____

One little thing I can do today towards it:

_____

_____

Vision for the day:

_____

_____

_____

Celebration & gratitude pause:

_____

_____

_____

Support note to myself:

_____

_____

Blank Slate Page:

Words are a lens to focus one's mind. — Ayn Rand

Date:_____ Personal Fuel Tank Rating (1-10): _____

Word(s) of the day or headline:

_____

_____

Today I desire:

_____

_____

Dream worth pausing for:

_____

_____

One little thing I can do today towards it:

_____

_____

Vision for the day:

_____

_____

_____

Celebration & gratitude pause:

_____

_____

_____

Support note to myself:

_____

_____

_____

Blank Slate Page:

There is only one thing that makes a dream impossible to achieve: the fear of failure. — Paulo Coelho

Date:_____ Personal Fuel Tank Rating (1-10): _____

Word(s) of the day or headline:

_____

_____

Today I desire:

_____

_____

Dream worth pausing for:

_____

_____

One little thing I can do today towards it:

_____

_____

Vision for the day:

_____

_____

_____

Celebration & gratitude pause:

_____

_____

_____

Support note to myself:

_____

_____

Blank Slate Page:

A word after a word after a word is power.
— Margaret Atwood

Date:_____ Personal Fuel Tank Rating (1-10): _____

Word(s) of the day or headline:

_____

_____

Today I desire:

_____

_____

Dream worth pausing for:

_____

_____

One little thing I can do today towards it:

_____

_____

Vision for the day:

_____

_____

_____

Celebration & gratitude pause:

_____

_____

_____

Support note to myself:

_____

_____

Blank Slate Page:

You can make anything by writing. — C.S. Lewis

Date:_____ Personal Fuel Tank Rating (1-10): _____

Word(s) of the day or headline:

_____

_____

Today I desire:

_____

_____

Dream worth pausing for:

_____

_____

One little thing I can do today towards it:

_____

_____

Vision for the day:

_____

_____

_____

Celebration & gratitude pause:

_____

_____

_____

Support note to myself:

_____

_____

_____

Blank Slate Page:

Dreams don't work unless you do. — John C. Maxwell

Date:_____ Personal Fuel Tank Rating (1-10): _____

Word(s) of the day or headline:

_____

_____

Today I desire:

_____

_____

Dream worth pausing for:

_____

_____

One little thing I can do today towards it:

_____

_____

Vision for the day:

_____

_____

_____

Celebration & gratitude pause:

_____

_____

_____

Support note to myself:

_____

_____

_____

Blank Slate Page:

We are not human beings with a spiritual life, rather we are spiritual beings with a physical life. — Teillard de Chardin

Date:_____ Personal Fuel Tank Rating (1-10): _____

Word(s) of the day or headline:

_____

_____

Today I desire:

_____

_____

Dream worth pausing for:

_____

_____

One little thing I can do today towards it:

_____

_____

Vision for the day:

_____

_____

_____

Celebration & gratitude pause:

_____

_____

_____

Support note to myself:

_____

_____

Blank Slate Page:

It isn't what happens to you that is important, it is what you do about it that makes the difference. — W. Mitchell

Date:_____ Personal Fuel Tank Rating (1-10): _____

Word(s) of the day or headline:

_____

_____

Today I desire:

_____

_____

Dream worth pausing for:

_____

_____

One little thing I can do today towards it:

_____

_____

Vision for the day:

_____

_____

_____

Celebration & gratitude pause:

_____

_____

_____

Support note to myself:

_____

_____

Blank Slate Page:

When you stop having dreams and ideals – well, you might as well stop altogether. — Marian Anderson

Date:_____ Personal Fuel Tank Rating (1-10): _____

Word(s) of the day or headline:

_____

_____

Today I desire:

_____

_____

Dream worth pausing for:

_____

_____

One little thing I can do today towards it:

_____

_____

Vision for the day:

_____

_____

_____

Celebration & gratitude pause:

_____

_____

_____

Support note to myself:

_____

_____

Blank Slate Page:

The greatest discovery of my generation is that a human being can alter their life by altering their attitude.
— William James

Date:_____ Personal Fuel Tank Rating (1-10): _____

Word(s) of the day or headline:

_____

_____

Today I desire:

_____

_____

Dream worth pausing for:

_____

_____

One little thing I can do today towards it:

_____

_____

Vision for the day:

_____

_____

_____

Celebration & gratitude pause:

_____

_____

_____

Support note to myself:

_____

_____

Blank Slate Page:

If your dreams don't scare you, they are too small.
— Richard Branson

Date:_____ Personal Fuel Tank Rating (1-10): _____

Word(s) of the day or headline:

_____

_____

Today I desire:

_____

_____

Dream worth pausing for:

_____

_____

One little thing I can do today towards it:

_____

_____

Vision for the day:

_____

_____

_____

Celebration & gratitude pause:

_____

_____

_____

Support note to myself:

_____

_____

Blank Slate Page:

Honesty is the first chapter of the book of wisdom.
— Thomas Jefferson

Date:_____ Personal Fuel Tank Rating (1-10): _____
Word(s) of the day or headline:

_____

_____

Today I desire:

_____

_____

Dream worth pausing for:

_____

_____

One little thing I can do today towards it:

_____

_____

Vision for the day:

_____

_____

_____

Celebration & gratitude pause:

_____

_____

_____

Support note to myself:

_____

_____

Blank Slate Page:

Rule your mind or it will rule you. — Horace

Date:_____ Personal Fuel Tank Rating (1-10): _____
Word(s) of the day or headline:

_____

_____

Today I desire:

_____

_____

Dream worth pausing for:

_____

_____

One little thing I can do today towards it:

_____

_____

Vision for the day:

_____

_____

_____

Celebration & gratitude pause:

_____

_____

_____

Support note to myself:

_____

_____

_____

Blank Slate Page:

It may be that those who do most, dream most.
— Stephen Butler Leacock

Date:_____ Personal Fuel Tank Rating (1-10): _____

Word(s) of the day or headline:

_____

_____

Today I desire:

_____

_____

Dream worth pausing for:

_____

_____

One little thing I can do today towards it:

_____

_____

Vision for the day:

_____

_____

_____

Celebration & gratitude pause:

_____

_____

_____

Support note to myself:

_____

_____

Blank Slate Page:

Our lives improve only when we take chances.
— Walter Anderson

Date:_____ Personal Fuel Tank Rating (1-10): _____

Word(s) of the day or headline:

_____

_____

Today I desire:

_____

_____

Dream worth pausing for:

_____

_____

One little thing I can do today towards it:

_____

_____

Vision for the day:

_____

_____

_____

Celebration & gratitude pause:

_____

_____

_____

Support note to myself:

_____

_____

Blank Slate Page:

You are never given a dream without also being given the power to make it come true. You will have to work for it, however. — Richard Bach

Date:_____ Personal Fuel Tank Rating (1-10): _____

Word(s) of the day or headline:

_____

_____

Today I desire:

_____

_____

Dream worth pausing for:

_____

_____

One little thing I can do today towards it:

_____

_____

Vision for the day:

_____

_____

_____

Celebration & gratitude pause:

_____

_____

_____

Support note to myself:

_____

_____

Blank Slate Page:

If you create from the heart, nearly everything works; if from the head, almost nothing. — Marc Chagall

Date:_____ Personal Fuel Tank Rating (1-10): _____

Word(s) of the day or headline:

_____

_____

Today I desire:

_____

_____

Dream worth pausing for:

_____

_____

One little thing I can do today towards it:

_____

_____

Vision for the day:

_____

_____

_____

Celebration & gratitude pause:

_____

_____

_____

Support note to myself:

_____

_____

Blank Slate Page:

Without dreams, there can be no courage. And without courage, there can be no action. — Wim Wenders

Date:_____ Personal Fuel Tank Rating (1-10): _____

Word(s) of the day or headline:

_____

_____

Today I desire:

_____

_____

Dream worth pausing for:

_____

_____

One little thing I can do today towards it:

_____

_____

Vision for the day:

_____

_____

_____

Celebration & gratitude pause:

_____

_____

_____

Support note to myself:

_____

_____

Blank Slate Page:

Dream big. Start small. But most of all start. — Simon Sinek

Date:_____ Personal Fuel Tank Rating (1-10): _____

Word(s) of the day or headline:

_____

_____

Today I desire:

_____

_____

Dream worth pausing for:

_____

_____

One little thing I can do today towards it:

_____

_____

Vision for the day:

_____

_____

_____

Celebration & gratitude pause:

_____

_____

_____

Support note to myself:

_____

_____

_____

Blank Slate Page:

Be faithful in small things because it is in them that your strength lies. — Mother Theresa

Date:_____ Personal Fuel Tank Rating (1-10): _____

Word(s) of the day or headline:

_____

_____

Today I desire:

_____

_____

Dream worth pausing for:

_____

_____

One little thing I can do today towards it:

_____

_____

Vision for the day:

_____

_____

_____

Celebration & gratitude pause:

_____

_____

_____

Support note to myself:

_____

_____

Blank Slate Page:

Our deepest fear is not that we are inadequate, our deepest
fear is that we are powerful beyond measure.
— Marianne Williamson

Date:_____ Personal Fuel Tank Rating (1-10): _____

Word(s) of the day or headline:

_____

_____

Today I desire:

_____

_____

Dream worth pausing for:

_____

_____

One little thing I can do today towards it:

_____

_____

Vision for the day:

_____

_____

_____

Celebration & gratitude pause:

_____

_____

_____

Support note to myself:

_____

_____

Blank Slate Page:

Notes and Check-in Pages

Use these pages for periodic check ins, or additional space or notes for writing. How is journaling going over one week, month, or longer? What progress have you seen, individually or as a group? Note your observations, or simply use the space to write more.

Date:

Additional Notes or Check-ins:

Date:

Additional Notes or Check-ins:

Date:

Additional Notes or Check-ins:

Date:

Additional Notes or Check-ins:

Date:

Additional Notes or Check-ins:

Date:

Additional Notes or Check-ins:

References

Chapter 1

1. Staff. *VSL:SCIENCE // The two-minute plan for feeling better*. The Observer, March 2 2009. http://observer.com/2009/03/effects-brief-writing-health/ (Accessed November 16 2021).
2. Klauser, Henriette Anne. 2000. Write It Down, Make It Happen: Knowing What You Want – and Getting It! New York: Scribner.
3. Blackstone, Judith. 2012. *Belonging here: a guide for the spiritually sensitive person.*
4. Ram Dass. 1971. *Be here now, be here now, be here now, here be now, be nowhere now: remember.* San Cristobal, N.M.: Lama Foundation.
5. Wright, Judith, and Bob Wright. 2016. *The heart of the fight: a couple's guide to fifteen common fights, what they really mean, and how they can bring you closer.* p. 105, 108.
6. Lipton, Bruce. 2013. *The Honeymoon Effect: The Science of Creating Heaven on Earth.* Carlsbad, CA: Hay House. p. 75
7. 1 John 8:32 (NIV New International Version). 2011

Chapter 2

1. *Online Etymology Dictionary.* Douglas-Harper, 2021. Last modified 2021. https://www.etymonline.com/word/intention. (Last accessed November 17, 2021.)
2. Merriam-Webster, Inc. 2003. *Merriam-Webster's collegiate dictionary.* Springfield, MA: Merriam-Webster, Inc.

3. "Overview: Intention." *Oxford Reference.* Last modified 2021 https://www.oxfordreference.com/view/10.1093/oi/authority.20111006215902209?rskey=3mLcHh&result=19 (Last accessed November 17, 2021).

4. Wright, Bob. "Summer Leadership Training Living with Purpose Discussion." Lecture, Wright Foundation, Elkhorn, WI, June 22 2016.

5. Economy, Peter. *This Is the Way You Need to Write Down Your Goals for Faster Success.* Inc.com, February 28, 2018. Last modified February 28, 2018. https://www.inc.com/peter-economy/this-is-way-you-need-to-write-down-your-goals-for-faster-success.html (Last accessed November 17, 2021).

Chapter 5

1. Robbins, Jairek. *Gratitude and Happiness: The Science Behind Gratitude.* Last modified November 18, 2014. Accessed November 19, 2021. http://jairekrobbins.com/gratitude-and-happiness-the-science-behind-gratitude/ (last accessed Nov 19 2021).

Chapter 6

1. Wright, Bob. "AC72 Leadership Master's Capstone Discussion." Lecture, Wright Graduate University, Elkhorn WI, July 10 2016.

2. Wright, Judith, and Bob Wright. 2016. *The heart of the fight: a couple's guide to fifteen common fights, what they really mean, and how they can bring you closer.* P. 64

3. Ibid. p. 72-73

4. Ibid. p. 72

5. Wright, Judith, and Robert J. Wright. 2013. *Transformed!: the science of spectacular living.* Nashville, Tenn: Turner Pub. Co. p. 31

Gratitude

I would like to express my deepest thanks to those who helped me develop a love for journaling and produce this journal:

To my parents Rik and Candy, thanks for always buying me journals, and Drew for likely reading them.

Husband Sarab, thanks for your support and love.

Friends Betsy Wilson and Kris Wallingford, thanks for instilling the love of journaling in me from the first grade through college.

All my mentors, coaches and contributors to my own personal growth. It takes a village, and I am so grateful Drs. Bob and Judith Wright and the Wright and WGU community, Sage Lavine and the Women Rocking Business community, Samantha Skelly and the Pause Breathwork community, Michele Nevarez and the Beyond EI community.

To my allies and co-conspirators. To my clients past, present, and future. To my friends and loved ones.

Fans of journaling like you, who bring your curious mind to journal in service to your growth and transformation.

God and my angels, once again you have my back. I am eternally grateful for your love and support.

Thank you, I love you. Thank you, I love you. Thank you, I love you.

About the Author

Rachael O'Meara is a transformational leadership and executive coach who supports leaders to get out of overwhelm and reach their potential. For thirteen years, Rachael's experience in sales and client services at Google helped her have a pulse on what it takes to be a successful and thriving leader. She writes regularly for sites including Thrive Global, leads workshops in breathwork, and speaks on the practice of pausing to feel more empowered, focused and impactful at work and beyond.

Her book Pause was named one of 2017's top business books for your career and was featured in the New York Times, WSJ.com and on the TEDx stage. She received her Master's Degree in Transformational Leadership and Coaching from the Wright Graduate University in 2020, and also has an MBA from Fordham University. She is also an Associate Certified Coach (ACC) from the International Coaching Federation. Rachael lives in San Francisco and Sarasota, FL with her husband and pauses as much as possible to ski, road bike, and BE - a lifelong challenge.

www.rachaelomeara.com
facebook.com/groups/bethepause
Instagram: @Rachael_OMeara

Made in the USA
Columbia, SC
24 August 2023

21989703R00130